MW01014583

Drones, Drones, Everywhere! / Ashlee Cooper and Faye Paige Edwards
JUVENILE NON-FICTION
Cataloging-in-Publication Data is on file with the Library of Congress.
Printed in the United States of America
ISBN: 9798374107548
Imprint: Independently published

The artist used Adobe Photoshop to create digital illustrations for this book.

First Edition

DRONES, DRONES, EVERYWHERE!

Ashlee Cooper
Faye Paige Edwards

Savannah's mom is a drone pilot,
and teaches others how to fly.
Amazed by what her mom can do
she asked if she could try.

A drone is a robot in the sky.
Propellers spin to lift it high.
Use a controller to make it fly.
There is no pilot seated inside.

PROPELLERS

CONTROLLER

So excited
to learn to fly,
she teaches friends
who stop by,
drone safety rules
of the sky.
Not too fast!
Not too high!

Her friends listen
to Savannah share
how drones are helpful
everywhere!

In classrooms students build, code, and fly with imagination...

Science, technology, engineering, and math, provide STEMulation.

Around the world
important packages arrive,
delivered by drones,
to a customer's surprise!

In an emergency,
drones fly with urgency,
quickly fighting fires
when buildings are higher.

In the wilderness
drones look around,
for a missing person
on the ground.

When structures reach up high,
drones act like eyes in the sky,
showing what to fix
as they fly by.

At drone soccer
eSport competitions,
girls and boys fly
in different positions.
Winning the championship
is their mission.

Drones race past
in streaks of light.
Racers wear FPV goggles
for first person sight.

Night-time drone shows
have spectacular lights.
Not quite like fireworks,
but magically bright.

In fields where farmers sow,
drones fly over to help them know,
which plants need
extra care to grow.

Drones help sell homes
big and small,
taking pictures
to show to all.

In schoolyards
students soon may see
a drone landing vertically.
What a fun ride it will be!

Ready to soar
to new heights?
Be a pilot like Savannah,
and enjoy the fun of flight.

Rules of the Sky

I Will

Fly lower than 400 feet

Fly slower than 100 mph (miles per hour)

Keep my eyes on my drone

Check to see where it is okay to fly

Never spy

Take the free FAA TRUST test for pilots who fly for fun

I Will Never Fly

Near a plane or airport

Over people

Near emergencies

If I don't feel well

Use this
QR code
to watch
Savannah fly

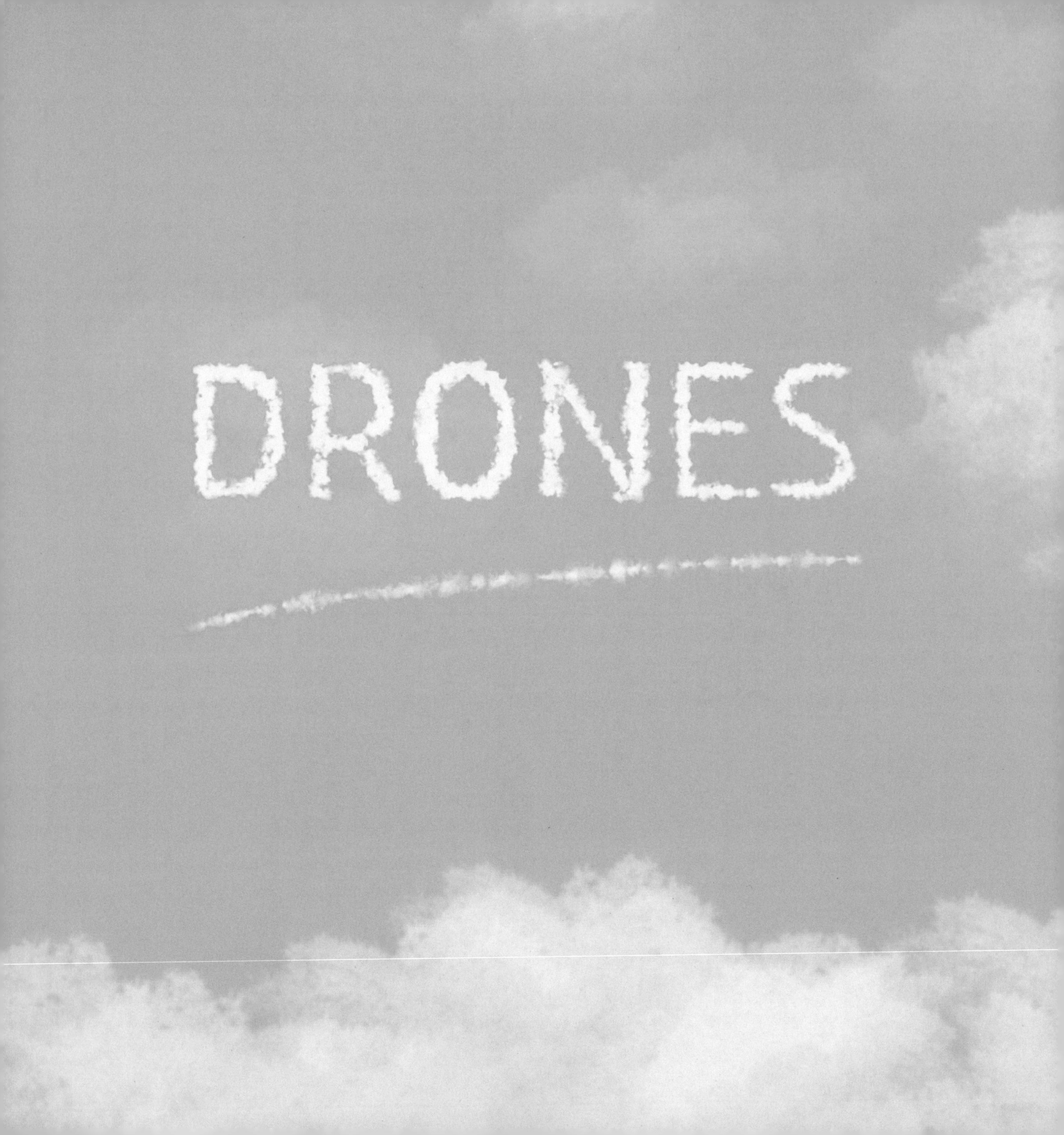
DRONES

More for Parents and Educators

Drones, Drones, Everywhere! introduces many ways drones (uncrewed aircraft systems) are used. Drone applications are rapidly expanding. Piloting skills open doors to many highly paid STEM, arts, and aviation careers, preparing students for their future jobs. There are even scholarships for eSports. The adventure continues with a **Glossary** and **"Let's Talk About Drones"** questions and answers.

Droneversity's STEMulation programs, camps, drone sports, and activities are designed for different learning environments and ages. They unlock the exciting world of technology. Professional development is also available for adults who want to bring flying robotic education to a school, community group, or organization.

All drone pilots are required to pass The Recreational UAS Safety Test (TRUST). It is free and can be taken at droneversity.org. To earn money flying drones, you are required to be 16 years old and pass the FAA Part 107 exam. Droneversity offers online and in-person exam prep courses for anyone looking to begin, expand, or change careers.

Glossary

Bird's-Eye	Seeing something from up high, like a bird
eSport	Short for electronic sports that use game controllers
Coding	Special instructions for a computer telling it to do cool things
Championship	The team or person who wins a game
Drone	A flying robot without a pilot sitting inside
Drone Soccer Ball	A drone protected from crashes by a round plastic cage
Emergency	A serious situation that is not expected
FAA	The Federal Aviation Administration makes sure the skies are safe
FAA-Certified	You passed a test for permission to make money flying a drone
FPV Goggles	Use a First Person View headset to see what drones see
Propellers	Spinning blades, like little fans, lift or push a drone into the air
Sow	Plant a seed in the ground
S.T.E.A.M.	Science, Technology, Engineering, Art, and Math
S.T.E.M.	Science, Technology, Engineering, and Math
STEMulation	Makes studying S.T.E.M. fun
Structure	Bridges, towers, schools, houses, and other buildings
Urgency	Needs your attention right now
Vertically	Moving up or down
Wilderness	A place far, far away from houses and people

Let's talk about drones!

What is your favorite picture in this book?
Why is it your favorite?
As a pilot, how will you use your drone?

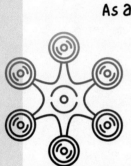

#1 What is a drone?

#2 How does a drone fly?

#3 Can drones have different shapes and sizes?

#4 How do drones help firefighters?

#5 How do drones help farmers?

#6 Do drones help find missing people?

#7 What is one safety rule you will follow when flying?

#8 What is a drone soccer ball?

#9 What is FPV?

Answers on next page

the answers!

#1 What is a drone?
A drone is a robot that can fly. It doesn't have a pilot inside. Someone on the ground uses a remote control. Some drones have cameras and other equipment to do special jobs like seeing if a plant needs extra care or spraying a fire.

#2 How does a drone fly?
When the pilot turns the drone on, the battery sends power to the propellers to make them spin. The battery is rechargeable, just like you charge a cell phone. Propellers are like little fans that spin around really fast. When the propellers spin, they lift or push the drone into the air. Two sticks on the controller tells the drone to go faster or slower, up or down, forward or backward.

#3 Can drones have different shapes and sizes?
Yes. Some are so small they can fit in your hand. Others are larger than a person! The shape of a drone depends on how you will use it. Some drones look like little helicopters. Others have a way of carrying packages.

#4 How do drones help firefighters?
Drones spray water and special liquids on fires.

#5 How do drones help farmers?
Drones take pictures from up in the air. This helps farmers see which plants are healthy and if any have bugs or are sick. Drones spray plants with special liquids to help make them healthier.

#6 Do drones help find missing people?

Sometimes, people are lost in places far away. It is not easy to find them. Drones fly high over a large area. Cameras on drones see people and things you can't see from the ground. One type of camera sees (or senses) the heat of a warm body of a person or an animal. This is especially helpful if someone is hurt or it is dark outside.

#7 What is one safety rule you will follow when flying?

- Do not fly too high
- Do not fly too fast
- Always keep my eyes on my drone
- Always check to see where it is okay to fly
- Never spy
- Never fly near a plane or airport
- Never fly over people
- Never fly near emergencies
- Never fly if I don't feel well
- Take the free FAA TRUST test for pilots who fly for fun

#8 What is a drone soccer ball?

The plastic around the drone helps it bounce off other drone soccer balls. Players try to knock the other team's drones away from the goal. They use a special controller to fly up and down, left and right, and even spin around in the air. Drone soccer balls fly very fast and are only flown indoors. It takes lots of practice to fly a drone well enough to play drone soccer.

#9 What is FPV?

FPV stands for "First Person View." You wear a virtual headset or goggles that make it seem like you are sitting inside the drone, but you are not. You see exactly where the drone is going and what it is seeing. FPV flying takes a lot of practice. It is used by drone pilots for racing, taking pictures from high in the sky, and many other applications. It's fun to be like a pilot inside the drone while standing on the ground.

ACKNOWLEDGEMENTS

I extend my heartfelt gratitude to the Droneversity team and my family for their encouragement and assistance in helping me become an author. Faye Paige Edwards, Droneversity's Solutionist, helped me envision a children's book about drones! My niece, Madison Rose Wells, served as Creative Consultant. Susie Paige, the first published author in our family, provided constant support. This is the team that made **Drones, Drones, Everywhere!** possible.

Becoming an FAA Part 107 pilot was life-changing. It has been a source of joy and success beyond the income from flying drones. This book is a testament to the endless possibilities achieved by utilizing all my passions and skills. I am forever grateful.

"Each of you should use whatever gift you have received to serve others, as faithful stewards of God's grace in its various forms." (1 Peter 4:10)

Pilot Ashlee Cooper

DEDICATION

To Savannah Rose,

My smart, beautiful girl. Before you could walk, I dreamed of the many ways you would soar. Watching you discover the wonders of aviation and STEAM has been one of the greatest joys of my life. You were my first drone student. I will always cherish the memories of teaching you to fly and code. As I take to the skies as a drone pilot and private pilot student, I am so happy for you to see it all. I am filled with excitement and pride as I think of the amazing things you will accomplish with all the resources available to you. Thank you for inspiring me to write this book and for being the light of my life. I love you forever and always.

~ Mommy

Pilot Savannah and
Pilot Ashlee Cooper,
Founder and CEO of
DRONEVERSITY

30122392R00021